Clay Play

A natural art method for young children. This clay method book can be used whether you are a caregiver, preschool teacher, art teacher, or parent. Children of all ages love to play with clay.

Learn more about this proven natural art method by reading -
Nurturing Children In The Visual Arts Naturally© methodology book ISBN 978-0-9916264-0-3.

Nature of Art For Kids® Publishing
P.O. Box 443
Solana Beach, California 92075

http://www.ecokidsart.com
email: treepassion@gmail.com
This book may be purchased for educational sales promotional use.

First Edition

Designed & Photographed by Spramani Elaun

Subject: Children's Art/Art Education

Table of Contents

Clay Play

By Spramani Elaun

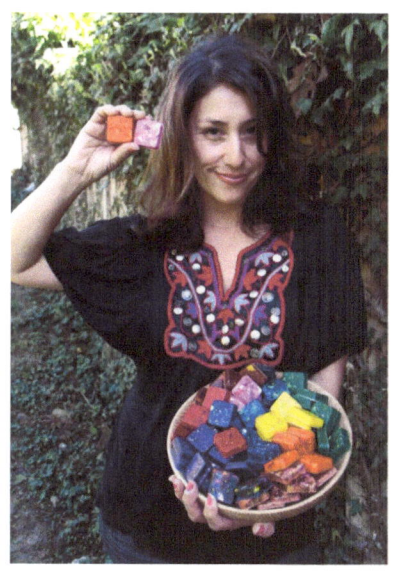

Working with children has been such a delight and an amazing journey. I've spent thousands of hours playing with clay alongside children of all ages. My path toward natural teaching began in the early 2000s. My focused, naturalistic observations on how children develop artistically is why I've decided to write this book and share this beautiful art experience I call Clay Play.

Opening

I start my morning setting up for class by laying out art supplies. I first open the bag of clay and a strong earthy scent looms out into my immediate air. It's musky, almost like wet dirt. I imagine this is what discovering an uninhabited cave would first smell like. It's a calming, natural scent that's not off-putting or harsh, just a good earth scent like the memory of mud pie making in my youth.

The clay is cool in temperature and I feel a slight residue on my hands. Its coolness is calming to me and sparks my sensory system right up. My head quickly fills with ideas for the kids to make, but I must resist the temptation to make any type of forms. I want the clay to stay unidentified! I want my students to get a sense of true natural exploration by my staged environment. It's the best way to bring natural discovery to the kids in an arranged time frame and moment.

I pull the red colored clay out of the bag, and it is heavy and dense. I divide the clay into chunks for each student that I'm expecting. I use hemp wire commonly, but if I can't find that, sometimes I just use yarn string or craft wire. Any of these types of string can glide through to cut pieces of clay. I halve, third, or quarter clay depending on how much I have and how many kids are coming.

I drop the cool clay onto the table spaces where I know the kids will gather. I carefully lay out tools like cookie cutters, wood modeling and cutting tools, rolling pins and containers with earthy embellishments for decorating the clay forms the kids will wildly make. I put a lot of detail into being sure the kids can reach the materials from all different angles of the table. I place wood twigs I collected off the ground for poking clay and maybe making small sculptures. Who knows where this will lead? Every set of students is different and I'm always amused by how creative kids get with these natural elements.

I wait for the festival of discovery as the children arrive one at a time. The first thing that happens, which I can always count on, is that a child will rush to the table and a parent will quickly remind them to wait for the teacher to tell them what to do. Usually the adults back them away from the table. At that moment, I calmly drop to the level of the table and encourage the kids to touch and discover the clay lying on the table, saying there is no need to wait. I start to poke and describe simple facts about the clay but give no instructions on what to make with it yet. I softly explain my natural art method and ask the adults to step back and allow the child's natural reactions and movements. I instruct the adults to take their own clay and feel and touch without speaking. The children's eyes are wide and curious and even more so are the adults around the table as they quietly take my cue and explore the clay and wait for what my natural method will lead to next. I notice deep reflective glances on the parents' faces as they watch their children discover clay naturally for the first time.

Clay Is Malleable and Easy For Young Hands

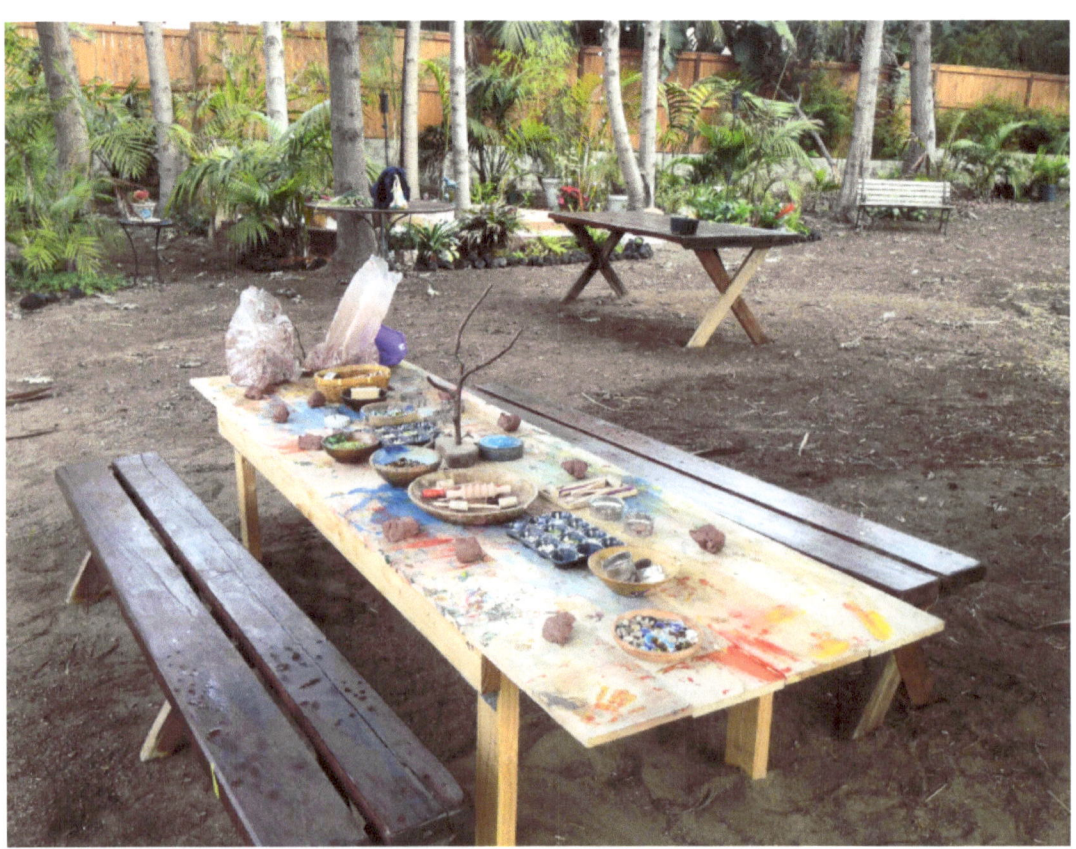

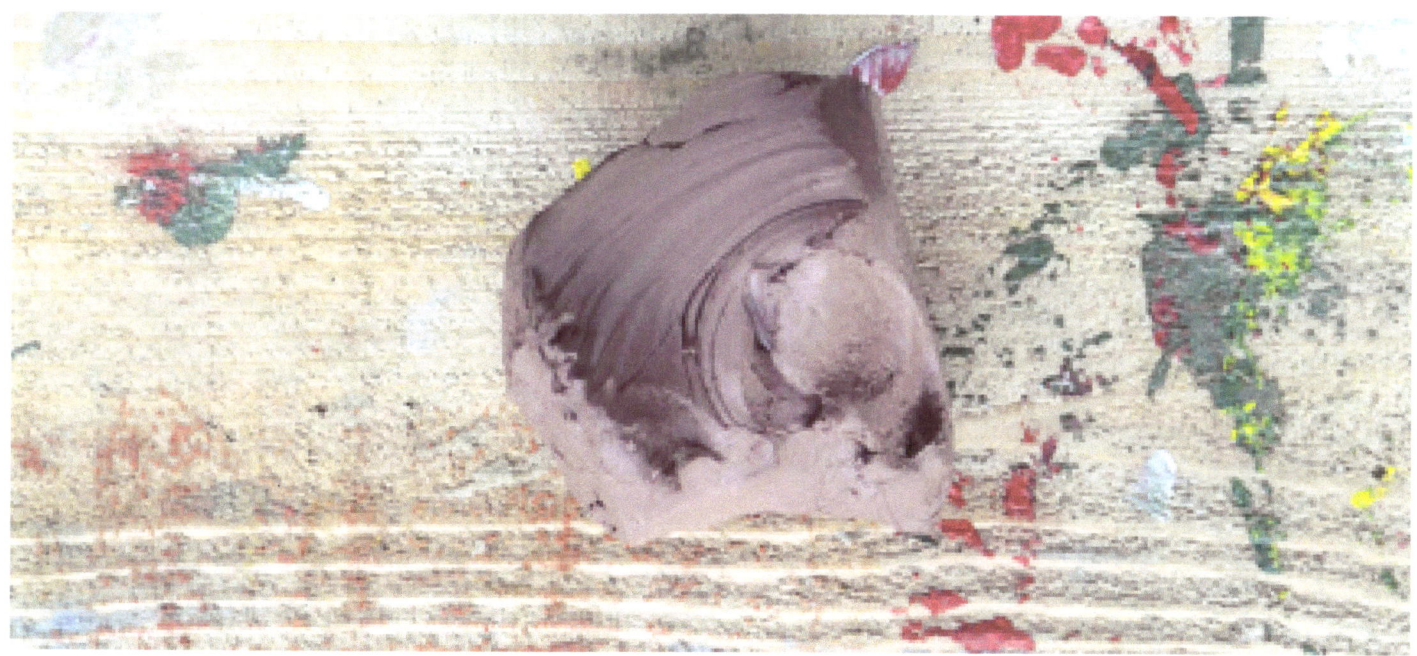

Exploring through clay play

To a young child, exploring through clay play is simply natural. Children collect knowledge and gain a sense of their physical world through their senses of seeing, smelling, tasting, touching, and hearing. The excitement a child experiences while pinching, rolling, patting, squeezing, or modeling clay is a curious mixture of the senses! Visual art exploration is a natural way for children to explore and learn and it can come in many forms: modeling, building, sculpting, and many other forms of visual art making.

Playing with clay is good for young children for many reasons:

- Touching clay is a positive sensory sensation for developing children.
- Clay is malleable and easy for little hands to manipulate and form.
- Children see an unidentifiable mass form into their own ideas.
- Clay is a calming activity for children.
- Tearing away at clay and pinching it apart is a very curious process that is healthy.
- Clay modeling is so much fun!

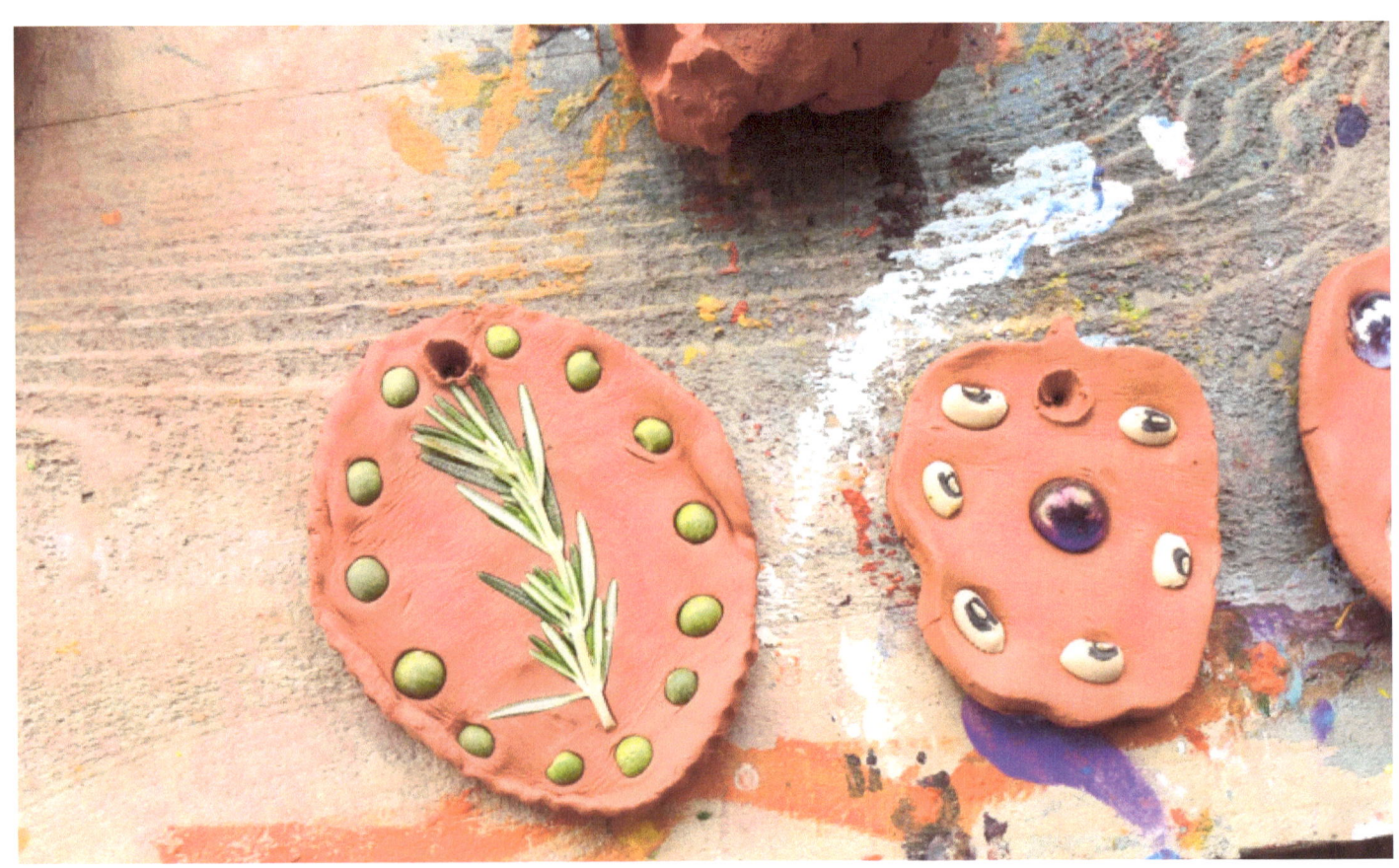

Clay Play - A Nurturing Method of Forming & Modeling Clay

This method is naturalistic because it is non-systematic and non-intentional. The method works along with a child's naturally developing sensory system and growth rate. Your role as mentor, art instructor, parent, or caregiver is to provide and select art experiences that freely allow intuitive thinking while exploring or making art, allowing the child's ideas and creative expression to flourish with no boundaries. Preparing the environment for these holistic clay play experiences to take place is important.

Clay Play is not far from methods learned in contemporary sculpture and ceramics today. Clay Play is my natural alternative to introducing clay forming and modeling in the younger years. It aligns with the child's growth, allowing the child to achieve skills in a safe environment without focusing on the end form, yet always influencing the child to develop artist skills while exploring the process of creating. Earth clay can be formed in different ways; the easiest way for a young child is by hand. Young children have the fine-motor capabilities to do most skills presented in this book, or can achieve these hand building skills with practice.

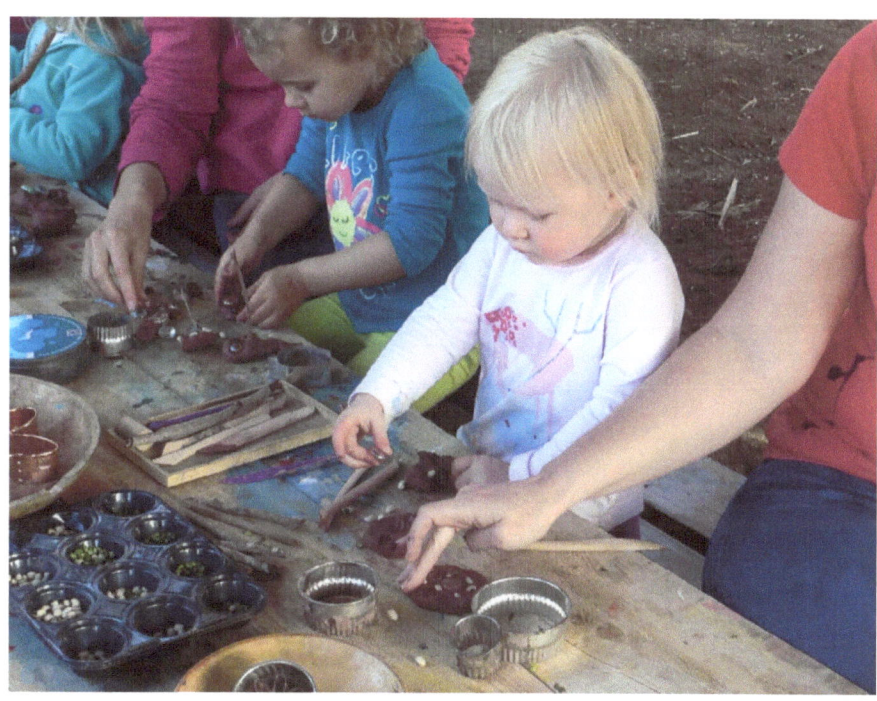

If you would like to learn more about the principals of this nurturing method, I recommend you read - Nurturing Children In The Visual Arts Naturally© 2014 book.

Clay Play is safe to explore at young ages

Children in this phase of their life, usually up to age three, still use their mouth as a sensory detector to explore objects. At this point, most primary caregivers provide snacks, finger foods, and safe toys that can safely touch the child's mouth without concern. This is the reason why young children stick everything into their mouths - they are not yet aware of objects with potential danger. This is the leading reason why a majority of caregivers believe small children are too young to explore visual arts. However, these ages are wonderful to start and I typically do start at these ages. Preparing the environment with safe supplies can be accomplished with good planning and appropriate fine motor projects. This phase is a great primer for visual art introduction with lots of positive tactile experiences that lead to healthy cognitive processing.

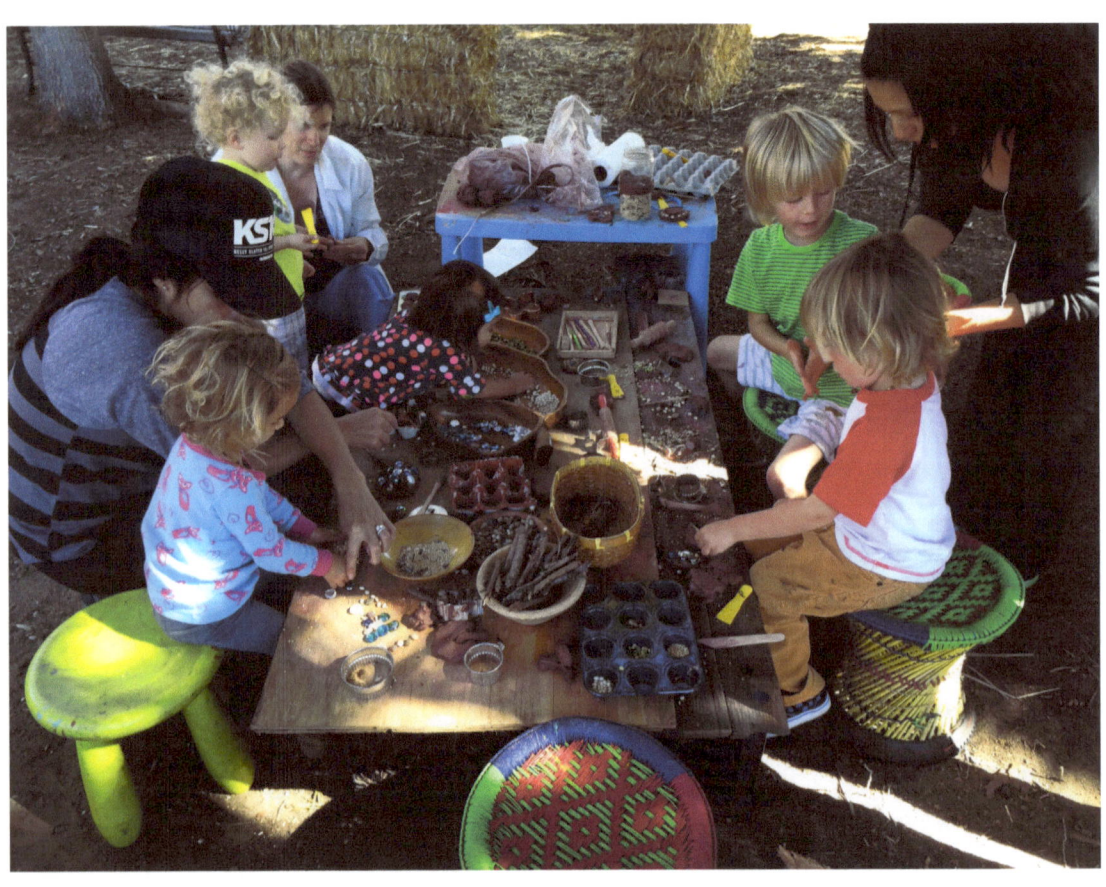

When Children Are Ready For Modeling Lessons

For children to be ready for modeling lessons, they must be mature in three developmental skills. In my book, Nurturing Children In The Visual Arts Naturally© 2014, I identity the three Component Skill Parts that affect how children learn and what makes them ready to visually communicate. The three parts are: 1. Cognitive Processing; 2. Visual Perception; and 3. Fine Motor Skills. I'm always looking at these three parts while a child explores or is making artwork. Monitoring these three parts helps me predict which phase a child is progressing through and how to nurture the natural structuralism of each child as I introduce visual art projects.

Ages 2 - 6

Based on the Component Skill Parts, I've discovered that children ages two - six are seeing and experiencing everything for the first time and don't understand the placement of visual arts in their young lives. Young children in this phase can't look at projects with planning. I recommend not introducing advanced modeling lessons and keeping it to basic forming shapes. Simple child-led projects are healthy for tactile learning. Free form making should be introduced, not complex clay forming. Cookie cutters, rolling pins, and wood modeling tools are good for tactile experiences. Plenty of hand manipulations while playing with clay are fun and great for fine-motor development. Average concentration time for this age is usually 20 - 40 minutes.

Ages 7 - 11

Children between ages seven - eleven are actively progressing in all three Component Skill Parts. Children at these ages have understanding of composition concepts and can follow guided directions. Exploring and imagination still play a dominant role in how artwork is made. Important exploration and curiosity is forming through this phase. Children want answers to cause and effect and look to visual art like scientific exploration at these ages. Three-dimensional child-led hand-building projects are perfect to introduce. Children are fine motor capable of mastering all forms presented in this book and can grasp beginning sculpting techniques. Introduce hand building projects like pinch pot making, coil methods, slab building sculptures, attaching forms, and carving out forms. Average concentration time for this age is usually 1 - 1.5 hours.

Curious Play

Curiosity is a quality related to inquisitive thinking such as exploration, investigation, and learning. This emotion represents a thirst for knowledge.

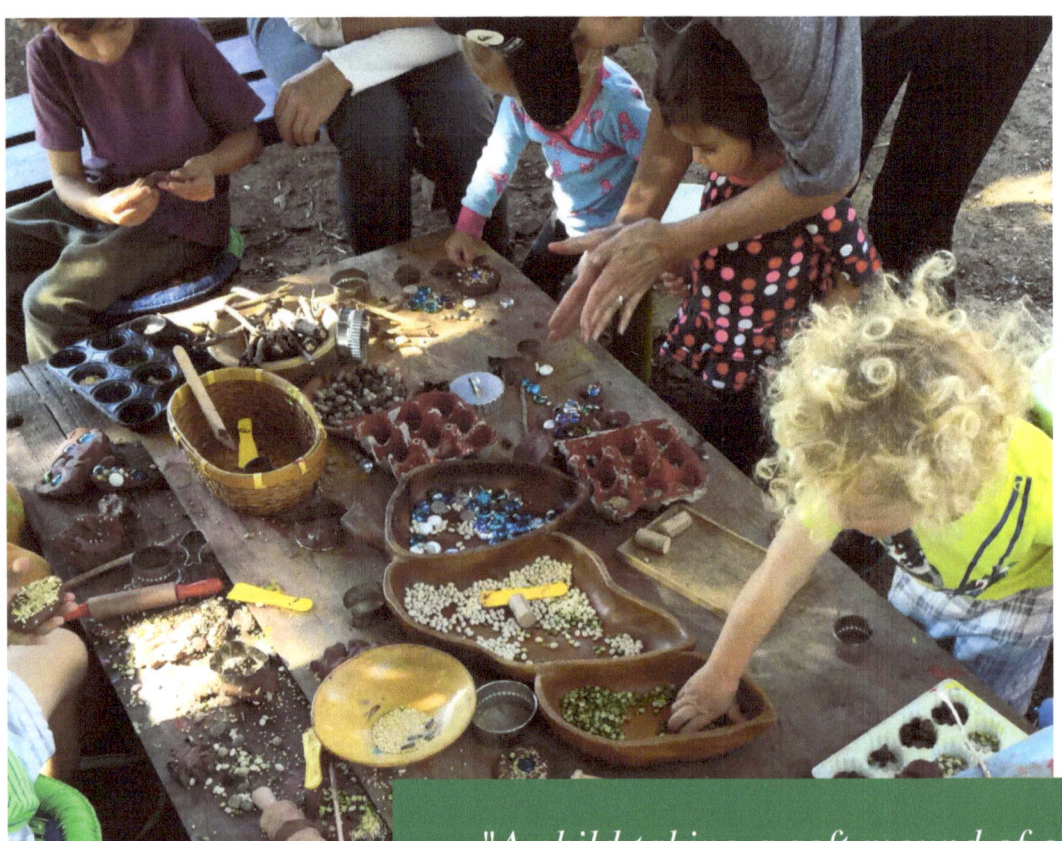

"A child taking a soft mound of clay into their own hands is a sensory feast for their eyes and hands."

Fine Motor Development Through Clay Play

Fine motor development is a physical attribute that advances as children grow. Fine motor control helps with creating art projects and using art materials. When fine motor control is achieved, a child can use a cookie cutter to cut shapes, smash or squeeze clay, roll ball shapes or model desired forms with their own hands. Getting fine tuned motor control takes years for young children, unlike adults.

A child gains motor development skills as he learns to control small muscles. These small muscles can be in their fingers, hands, arms, and even muscles around the eyes. Once a child achieves control of these small muscles, it becomes easier to learn art skills and explore techniques. Gaining mastery with movements can help with applying and adjusting pressure, pressing, pushing, and manipulating clay into a form. These movements become possible with full control of muscles. Just like with other large muscles, the more you use them, the more you have better control over them.

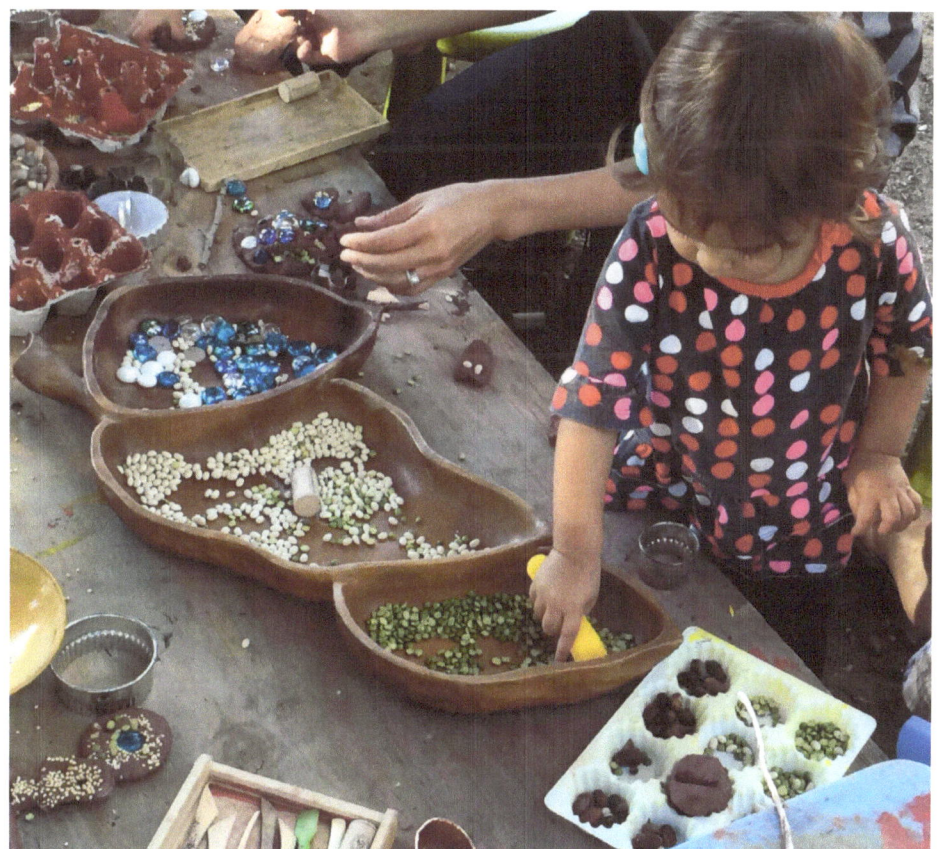

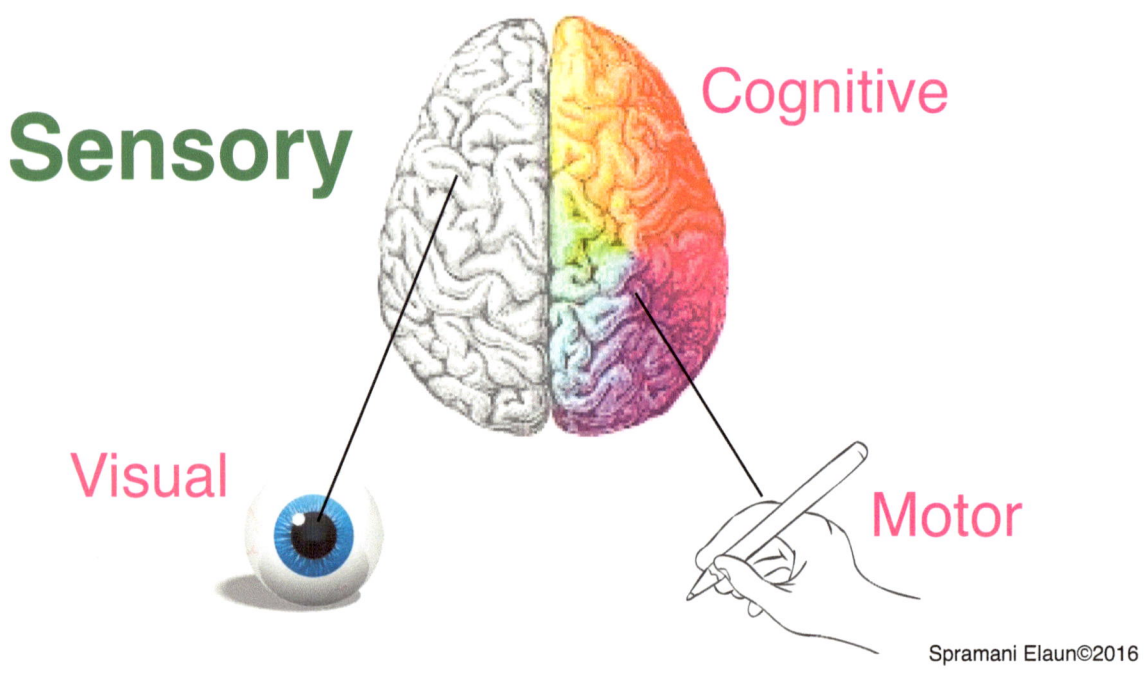

Sensory

Cognitive

Visual

Motor

Spramani Elaun©2016

Tactile Learning By Sensory Touch

Tactile learning can be described as learning through touching with one's own hands. When a child touches an object, messages of information are sent through sensory nerves to the brain. Tactile sensory sensations can help young children learn and understand ideas. Visual art learning can happen from direct sensory touching by hands. Tactile art making stimulates learning in different ways than visual or audio learning. For a developing child, tactile exploring can also lead to better fine motor function and control. Tactile learning is recommended for highly active children or those with kinesthetic learning styles. These types of children learn better by physical action and tactile sensations. Visually impaired children greatly benefit by tactile learning sensations. A child's clay manipulations or artwork are a representation of their understanding from tactile experiences.

It is very important for young children to experience sensory tactile art exploration. I recommend providing lots of tactile art experiences. Try out many different sensory art projects that can aid in learning and be experienced by hand manipulations. Provide lots of blocks of time for using hands and fingers directly.

> *"A child playing with clay can be transformed into a relaxed, meditative state!"*

Playing with clay can relieve stress

Why is playing with clay a calming or relaxing activity? Because touching clay induces stimulating neural input from most of our sensory senses. When a young child starts touching, forming, or modeling, it's considered active learning. Playing with clay stimulates tactile input, visual pathways communicate with both left and right hemispheres of the brain, and auditory and smell sensory systems are also collecting information. Playing with clay causes a high visual-auditory connectivity in the brain. Strong connectivity occurs and the child becomes intensely focused on his handwork. Children using their hands can be so engaged that other stress related thoughts clear their minds. The electrical activity stimulated in the brain becomes a different type of action, firing connections and allowing children to focus on their handwork only. A calming effect takes place because cognitive processing is occurring while forming or manipulating clay. It's good for children during their sensitive periods to develop good habits and activities that can help early in life to regulate relaxation by creative handwork.

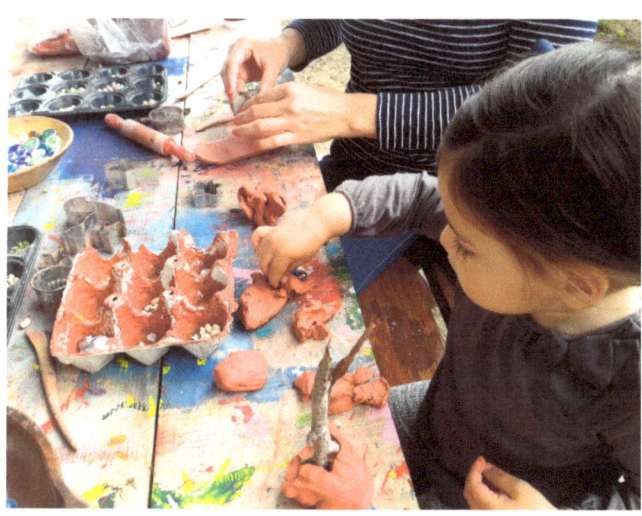

Art making is powerful & therapeutic

Artwork can speak volumes for a child, beyond communicating through speech. A child's reason for art making can come from a number of reasons: imagination, curious exploration, a past recollection, or even what is presently on a child's mind. For a child who finds it hard to talk, working with clay gives the power to communicate with only their hands. Children who can't verbalize well can express emotions, including sad, happy, imaginative, creative, and even painful feelings, through art making. Playing with clay can be therapeutic for children suffering from mild to extreme cases of emotional issues.

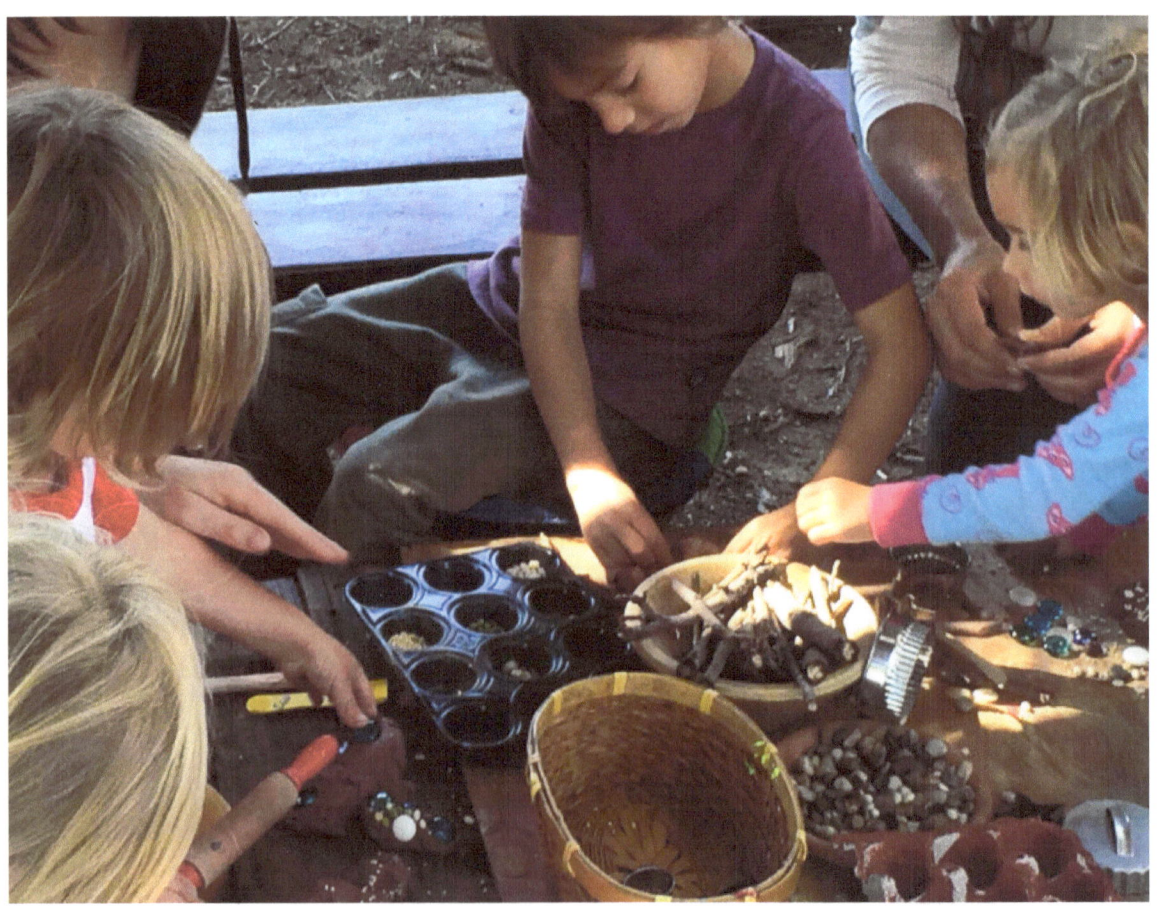

Art's Positive Link to Nature & The Environment

Over the years of developing my earth-friendly art lessons, I've had amazing observations present themselves. I have been able to observe links between children making art and becoming aware and conscious of their surrounding environment, specifically working with raw natural materials while creating art and craft projects. Raw materials include clay, natural wool, felt, twine, beeswax, natural plant pigments, stones, wood, twigs, natural fibers, handmade paper, and other interesting materials. The common link is that when children work with natural materials, it almost always leads to deep levels of thought and discussions about the planet's resources and how things are made or manufactured. These discussions always create awareness about sustainability and current environmental issues. I'm always pleasantly surprised by how these conversations naturally evolve.

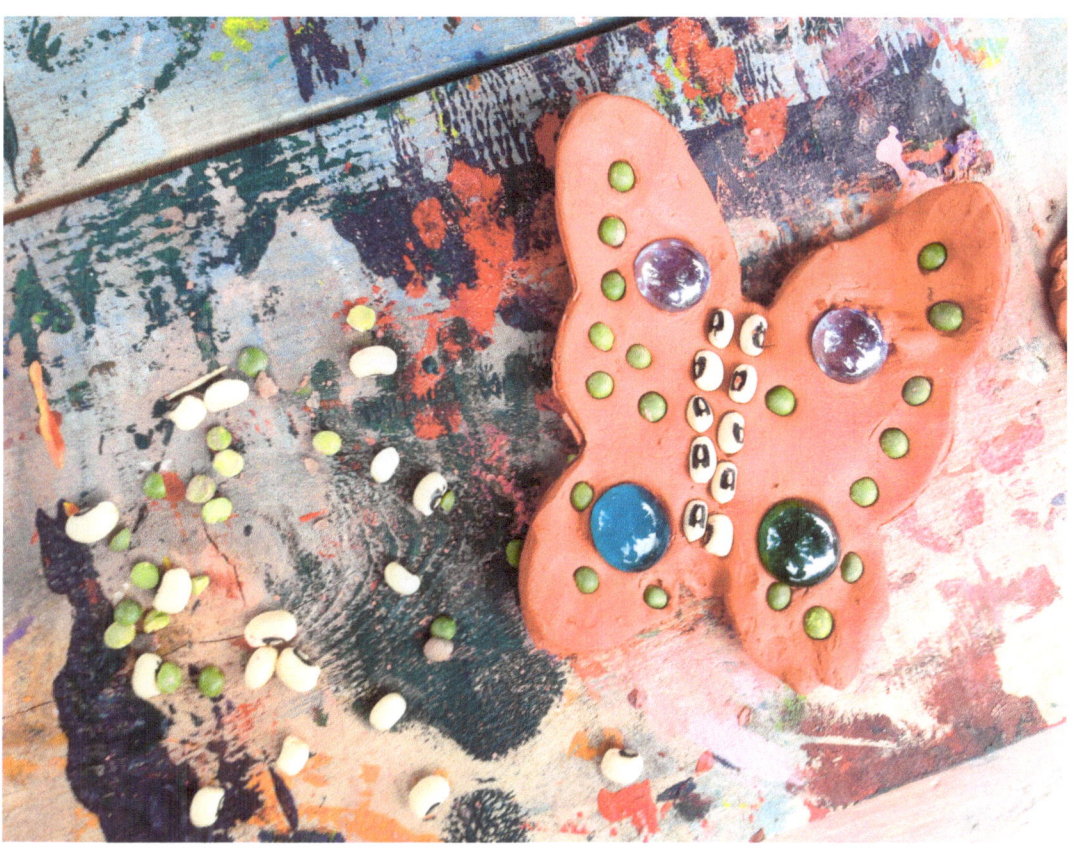

Dismantling Clay is Normal For Kids

It's quite common for a child to create a beautiful decorated form and later dismantle it or pick it apart afterwards. Believe it or not, dismantling and destroying clay is a learning process children need to experience. It's normal for children between the ages of two - six years to dismantle clay forms out of curiosity. These experiences help children have deep levels of thoughts and understand ideas. Playing with clay in this style can build strong foundations of under-standing their physical world. Dismantling clay can be just as important as the action of assembling clay forms. Children at these young ages are not overly concerned with producing an end product for display, but more so on the curious physical process and sensory stimulation they're learning from. It's important to clarify here that children at the same ages can possibly be at different logical and physical phases of development. All sequences of instructions can be the same but will never affect each individual child in the same way. This means that every child cognitively processes information differently, depending on their development stage in life, clay experience, or knowledge about clay forming. Older children have the abilities to create forms with an intention or plan and are less likely to dismantle their creations.

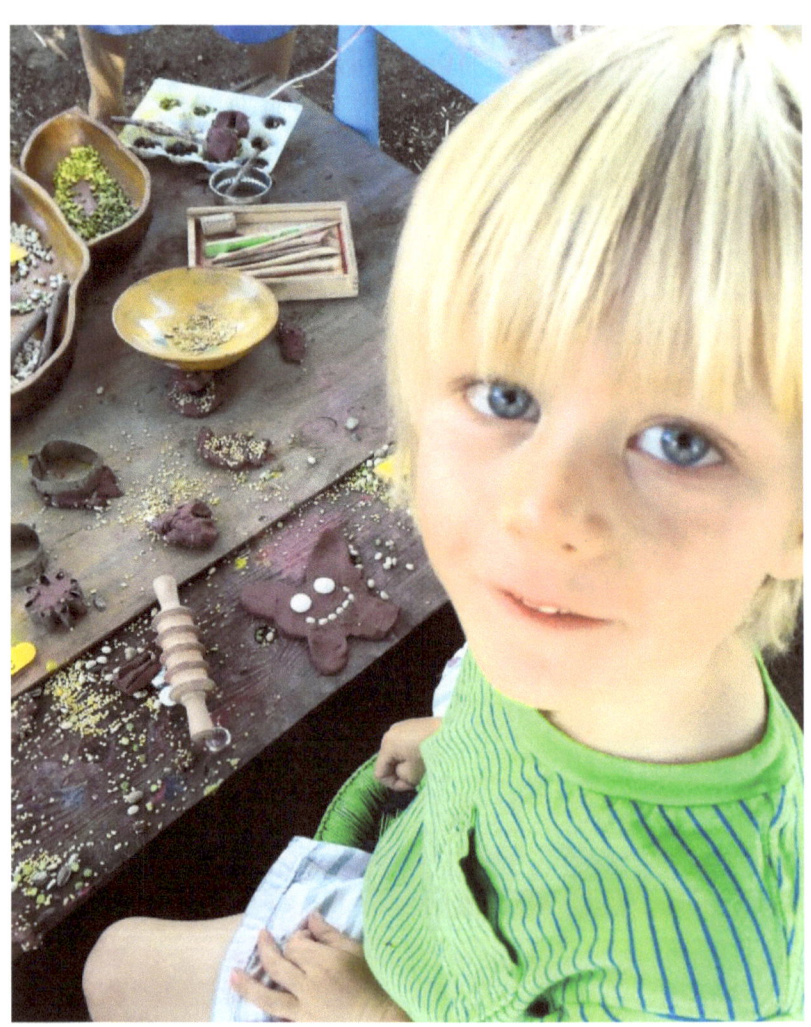

Tip: If your child creates a project you want to save as a keepsake, I recommend you quickly move it out of the reach of your busy little artist or dismantler.

Clay's Unpredictability Teaches Valued Lessons

Clay forming is unlike any other activity a child will normally do. Clay's malleable substance is a concept that children come to understand can create unpredictable results. Clay's soft physical structure and ability to harden takes some time to learn. After awhile, discovering clay's flexibility and witnessing it transform into a hard mass helps kids finally achieve predictable results. Frustration from failed attempts is part of that learning curve.

Example:

A child makes a small sculpture of his daddy with an oversized head too heavy to be supported by the body's base. After some time drying in the sun, the head breaks off the body. This unpredictability leaves the child feeling disappointed in his attempts at forming a body. But, this experience was very valuable

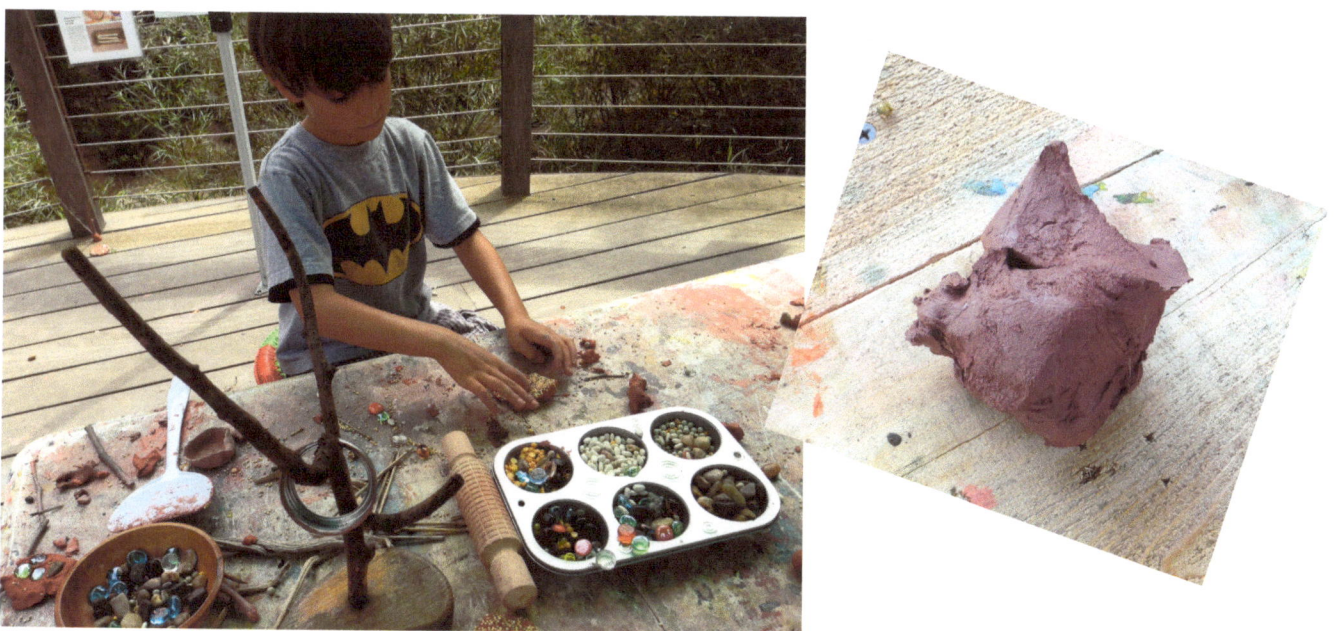

for understanding clay's process. Giving this child plenty of opportunities to form similar projects will help him understand clay's properties. When you explain or give helpful future guidance on building a base to hold a heavy top piece, the child will remember his past attempts. He will be able to meta-cognitively retrieve past memories of clay forming and apply his gained knowledge with skill. Making forms from soft malleable clay starts to make sense and the child gains techniques over time. This process can take years, depending on the child's stage in life.

It's good for a child to watch clay transform into predictable or unpredictable shapes. It's important not to put too much emphasis on planned forms or art projects. Most young children between ages two - six years are not fine motor capable and their visual perception and cognitive processing is in the beginning stages of development. Children seven - eleven years old are more capable of planned art projects.

Children expected to follow directions or planned projects can experience frustration and anger as a result of not being developmentally ready. Usually this occurs because the child can't control or predict clay's properties without experience. Young children should experiment and try techniques in a playful fashion, all driven by child-led imagination. This natural method of Clay Play is designed to align with a child's growth and be introduced as an exploratory process to discovery of modeling and forming.

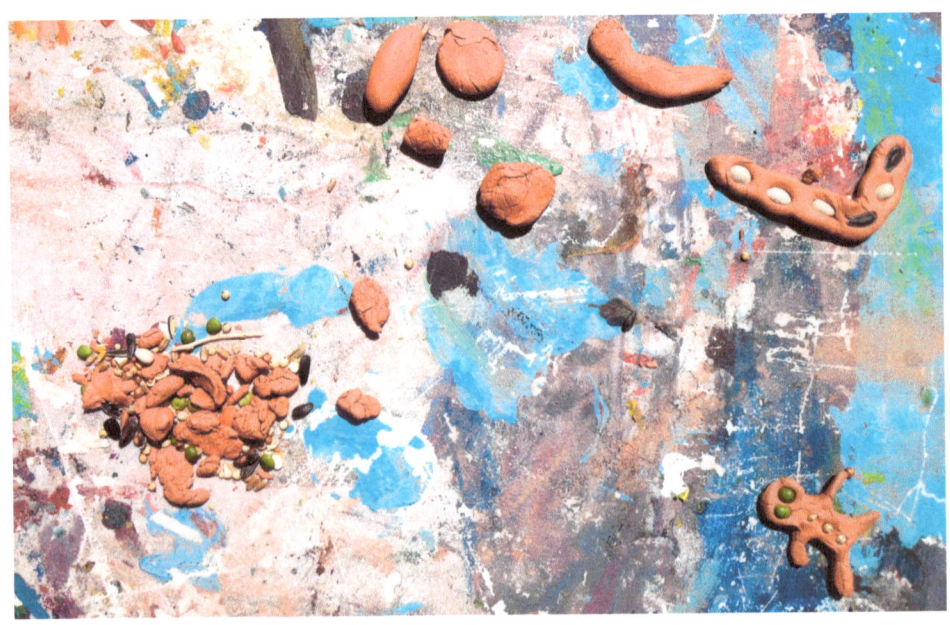

What is Air-Dry Pottery Clay?

Clay is part of the earth. Traditionally, red clay is used for making pottery and ceramics. Clay comes in many colors. When clay is baked, it turns into Terra Cotta, just like a terra cotta flowerpot. Terra Cotta means earth baked. For this activity, I use earthy tones like reddish brown air-dry clay. Earth clay is traditionally fired in an open fire, electric kiln, or gas kiln. For Clay Play, I recommend that you air-dry your child's forms. Setting clay forms in direct sunlight for a few days usually hardens them. Stove baking techniques can usually be found online or in ceramics technique books.

Where You Can Find Air-Dry Pottery Clay?

Commercial earth clay can usually be found in most craft-art or online stores. Clay can actually be found along native riverbeds and streams. Native clay will usually have debris, unlike smooth commercial clay. Raw, found clays can be prepared by shifting out debris. Shifting clay through a screen can remove small twigs, pebbles, or seeds. You can set it aside in a bucket to dry out to a workable moist consistency. Earth clay is very forgiving and it's easy to recycle scraps or undesired projects back into workable clay.

Use Only Non-Toxic Clay

Non-toxic clay has been tested by a toxicologist and is not harmful to your child's health if ingested, absorbed, or inhaled. A non-toxic label also ensures that the product does not cause acute or chronic hazards. U.S. labeling law requires that all companies selling or distributing art supplies in the U.S. must display the ASTM D 4236 code on their label, showing the product is non-toxic. Adult grade art supplies may not be safe for young children and have unsafe chemicals for young children. Be sure to read all safety information and warnings information on clay supplies. Young children should not spend large amounts of time in a commercial ceramic art studio due to the powders and dust that can be inhaled.

Air-dry to Bone-dry

Clay Play is tactile fine-motor movement play designed for kids to experience and process ideas through fun relaxed forming, rather than creating long lasting ceramics. Using air-dry pottery clay, which will become bone-dry when completely dried out. Bone-dry pottery clay does become extremely brittle and can break apart. Bone-dry clay can be fired in a kiln to harden and become long lasting if you choose. This method is not intended for you to follow-up with baking or firing, here you will only allow clay to become bone-dry for temporary artworks. Remember this method is for beginning young children to freely explore and go through the process of hand building. As children get older and more attached to their creations, I then recommend using air-harden type clays or firing bone-dry projects. When children master form and modeling techniques they are mature and ready for ceramic lessons.

You can find a local ceramic shop to bake artworks for long-term durability. I recommend checking in with a ceramic shop for specifications before kids make projects to go into a kiln to be fired. Please note the natural embellishments I recommend in this book cannot be fired.

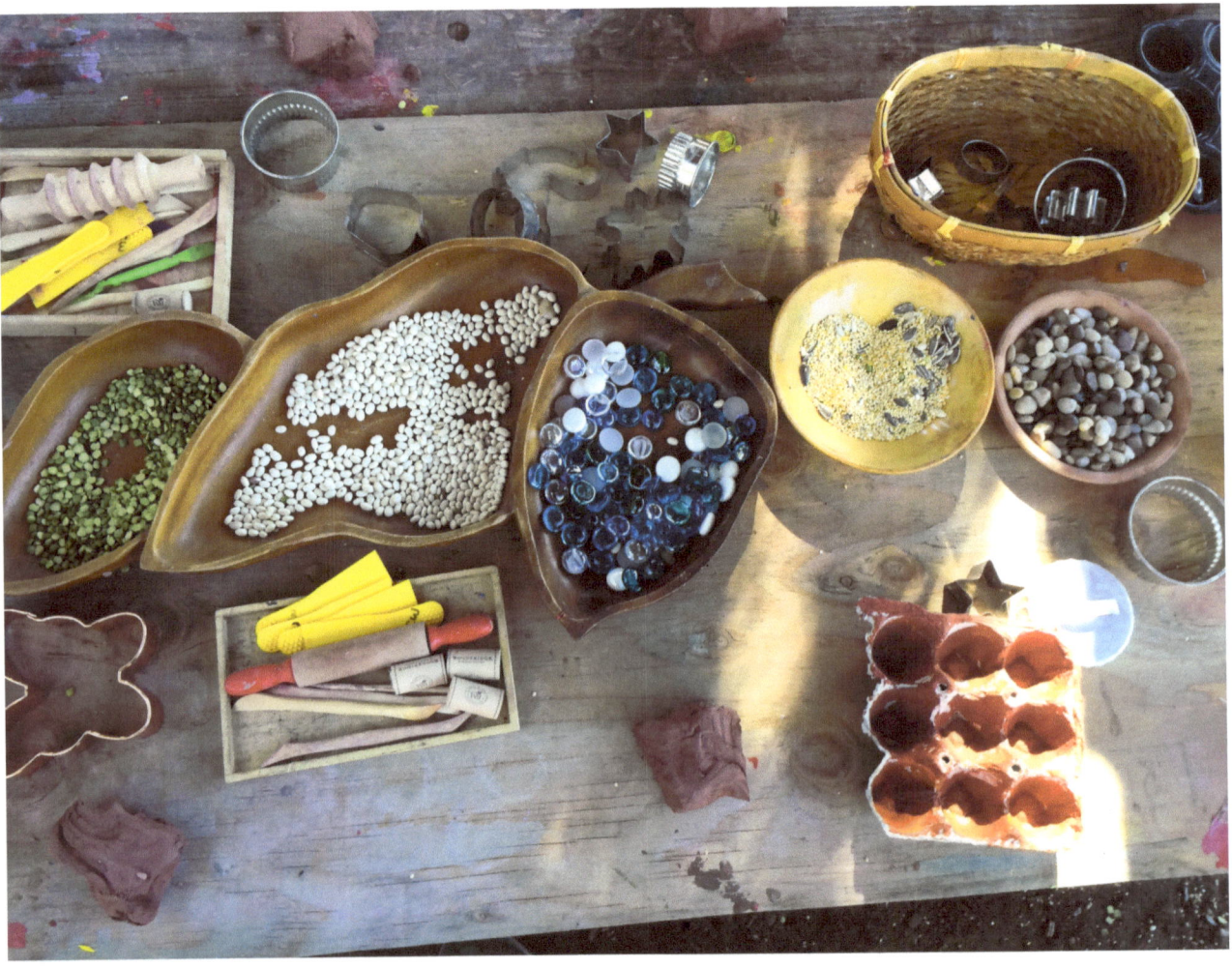

Keeping Clay Moist

Air-dry pottery clay dries quick. To make clay moist while working with it, use a spray bottle, wet sponge or just sprinkle water over drying areas with hands. Remember clay is very easy to revive and make malleable with just water. If you took all your child's dried out creations and socked them in a bucket of water you could recycle the clay for another time. Just like working with mud pies!

Drying & Storing Clay

Finished artworks should be placed somewhere they can dry out for a few days undisturbed. In direct sun is perfect, but indoors works too. Storing outdoors where its damp or possible raindrops will keep forms from becoming bone-dry. Also, remember projects can become brittle and make a mess after handling. They can become dry and crumbly like outdoor dirt.

Keep all air-dry clay stored in airtight containers or zip lock bags when not working with them. This keeps clay nice and moist and stops clay from drying out.

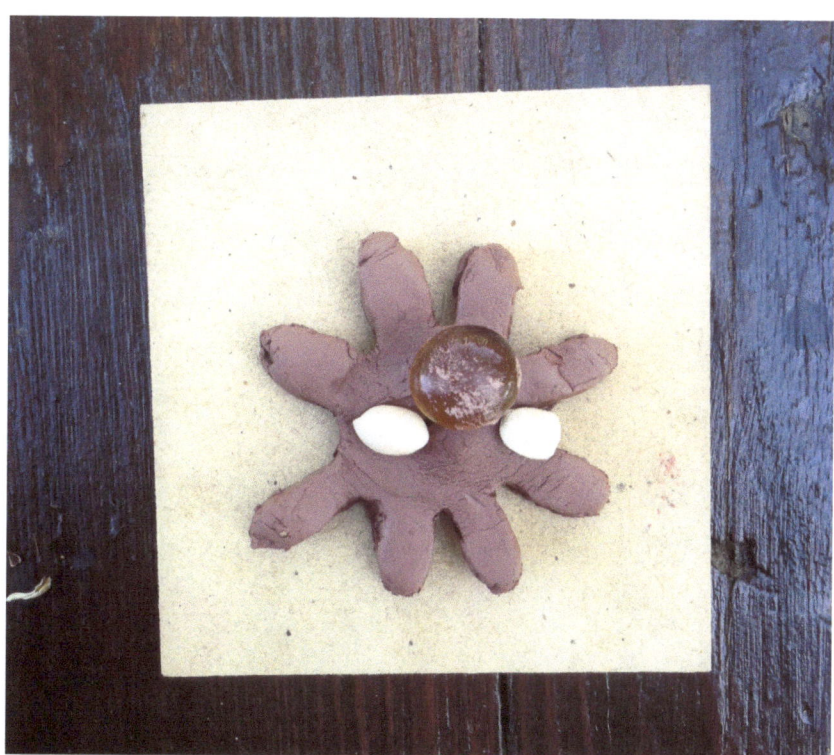

Seeds & Nut Embellishments

Seeds have been described by many natural artists as being exquisitely magical. Prickled, speckled, glossy, dry, round, or flat, they come in every size from tiny to pebble size. Seeds make beautiful natural embellishments in clay sculptures. Seeds can be gathered from backyard gardens and fields or found in any market.

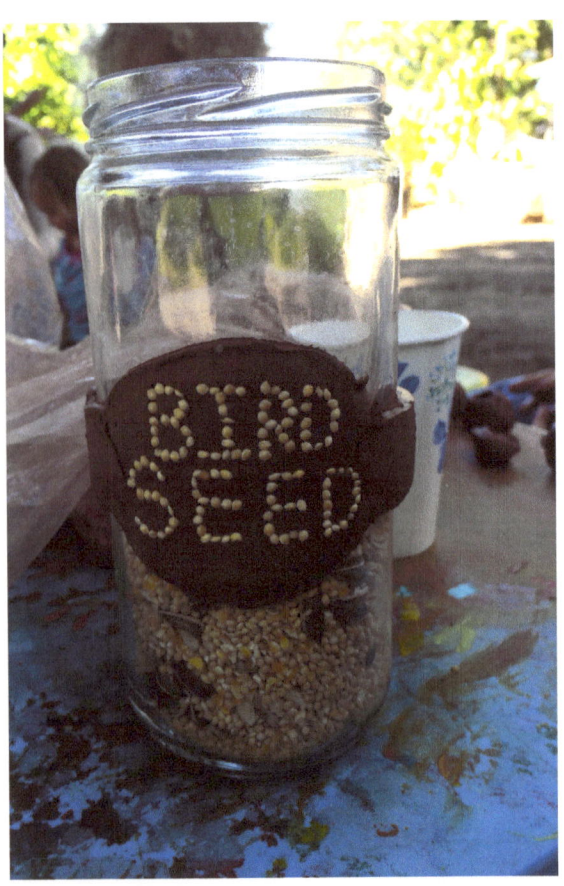

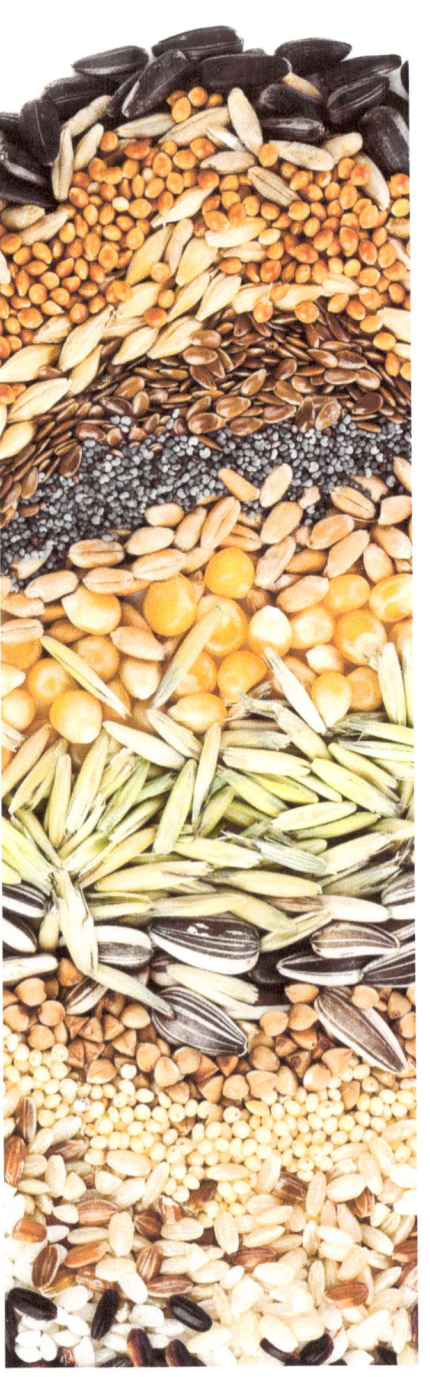

Sculpting & Carving Tools

Wood, plastic, or flat wire-ended clay carving tools in a variety of shapes; cookie cutters of any shape; wood board surfaces cut to any size for artworks to be stored on or carried out on; rolling pins; natural twine; twigs; a spatula; nickel wire or gardening wire for securing clay structures; and a clay metal scraper that can be used for sculpting.

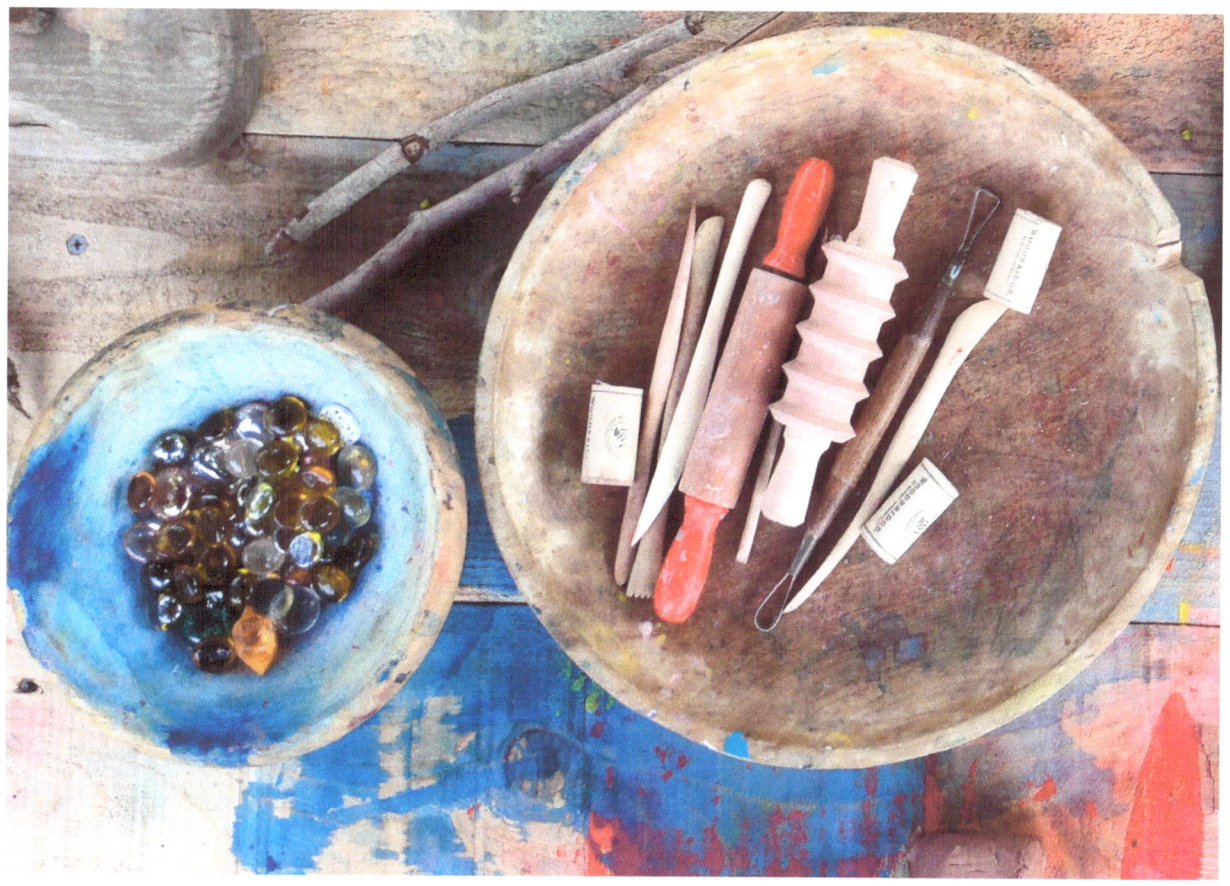

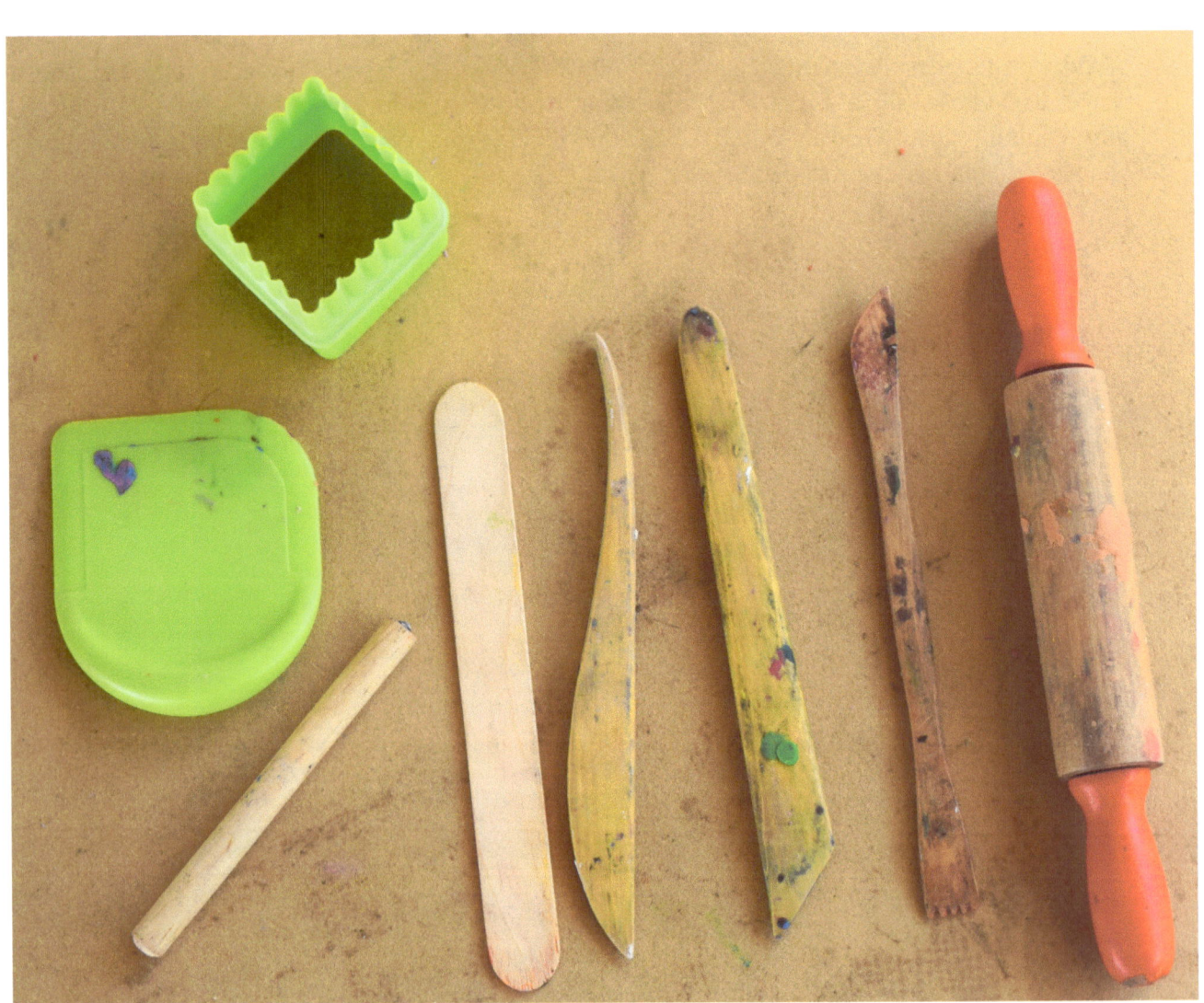

Gather fun decorating elements:

Glass Beads
Beans
Seeds
Herbs
Twigs
Pebbles

Caution!

Are you worried about young children putting small embellishments into their mouths? Keep it simple with clay, rolling pins, cookie cutters, and large twigs. Progress later when the child is past the stage of putting items into their mouth.

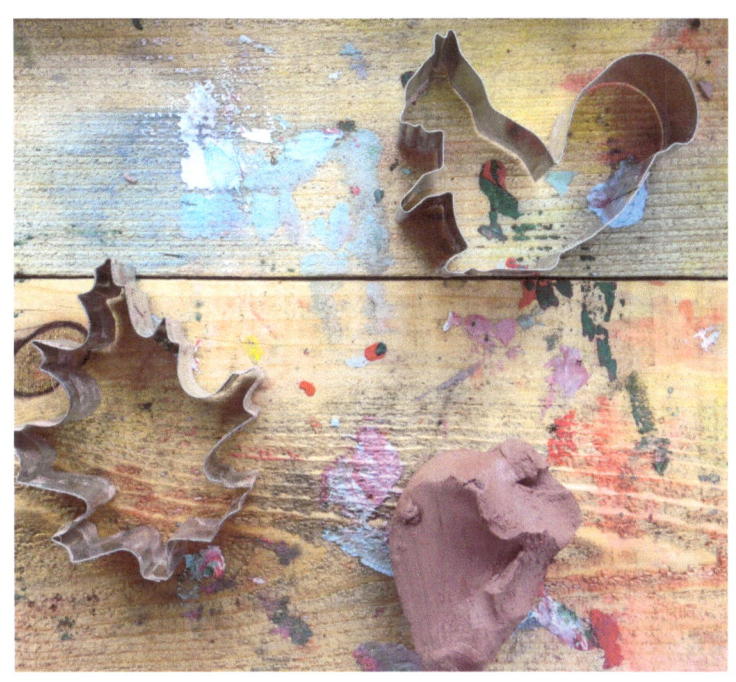

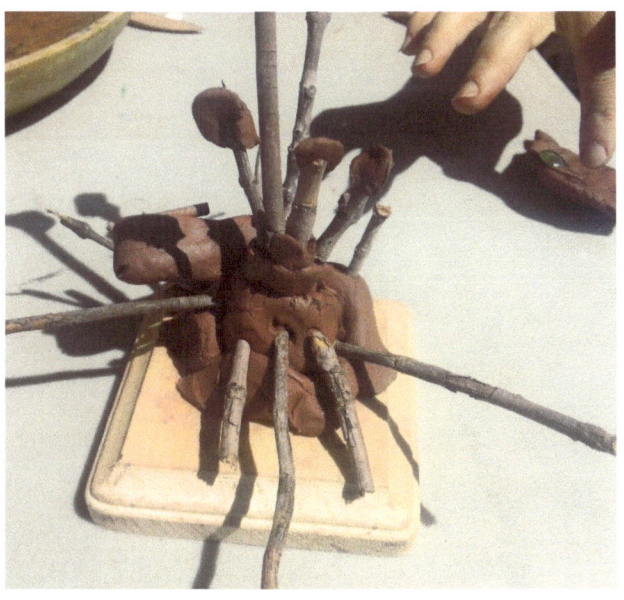

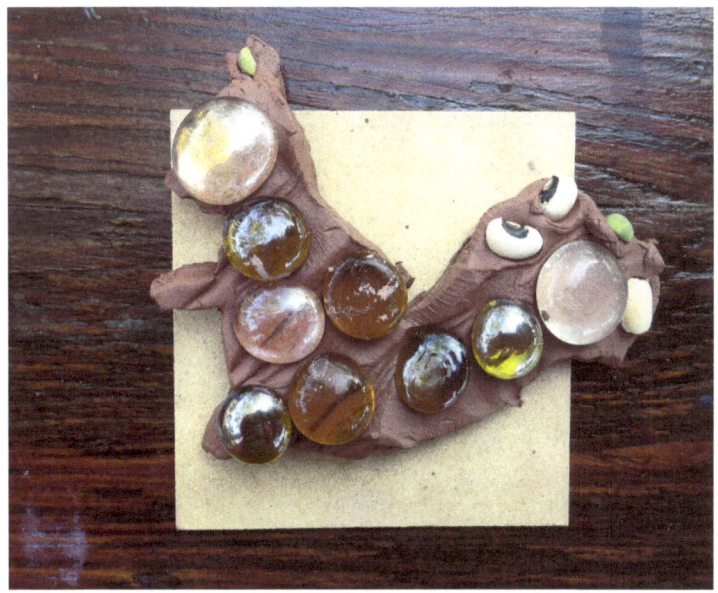

Teach Simple Movements First

Pinching
Squishing
Patting
Rolling balls
Back and fourth motion - rolling pin
Pressing
Poking
Tearing
Cutting & Slicing - wood modeling tool
Carving
Dig

Teach Simple Forms Second

Ropelike coils/ Snakes
Slab
Rounded and circular shapes
Mountain Peak
Cube
Cylinder
Pyramid/triangle
Tear Drop
Flat Pancake
Cookie Cutter Shapes

Older kids can learn to attach clay parts with carving tools, wire, tooth picks, and learn score and slip methods.

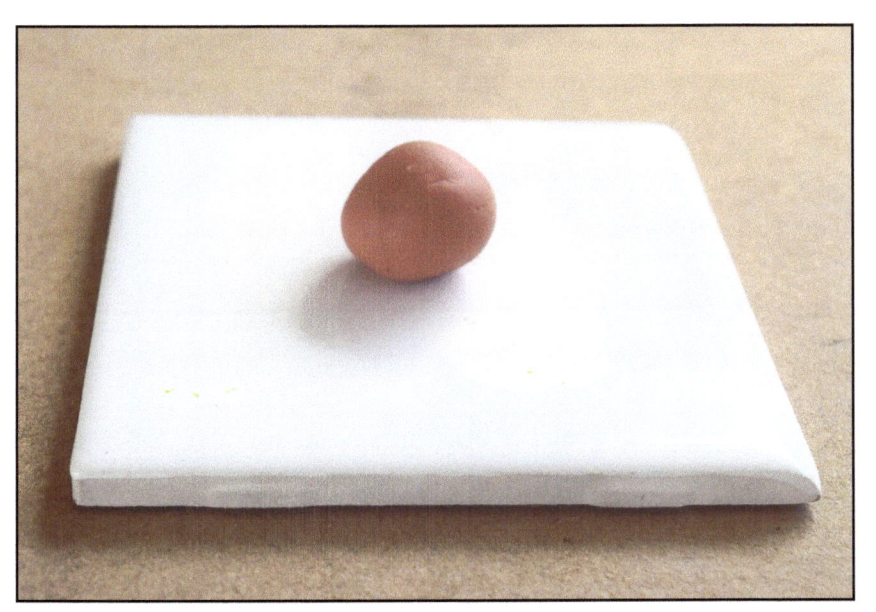

Rounded
Circular
Sphere

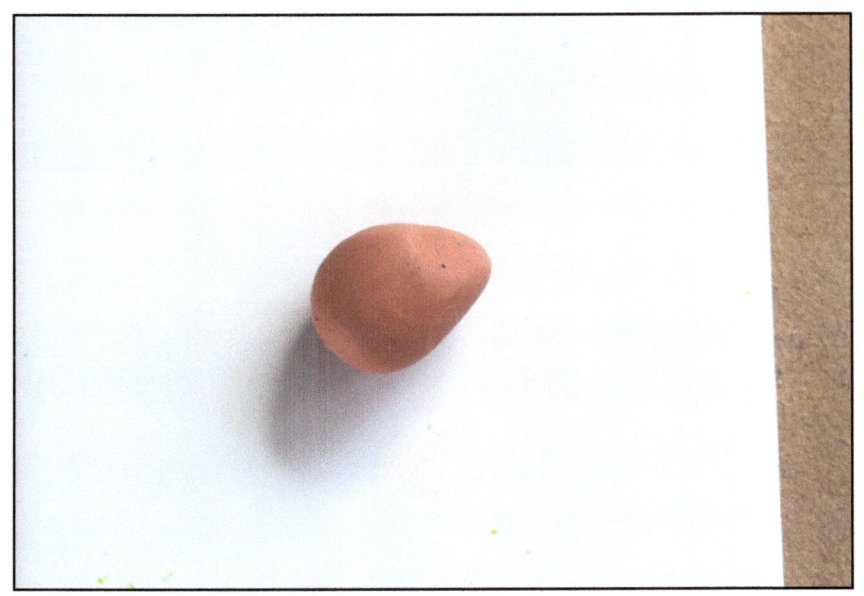

Tear Drop
& Oval

25

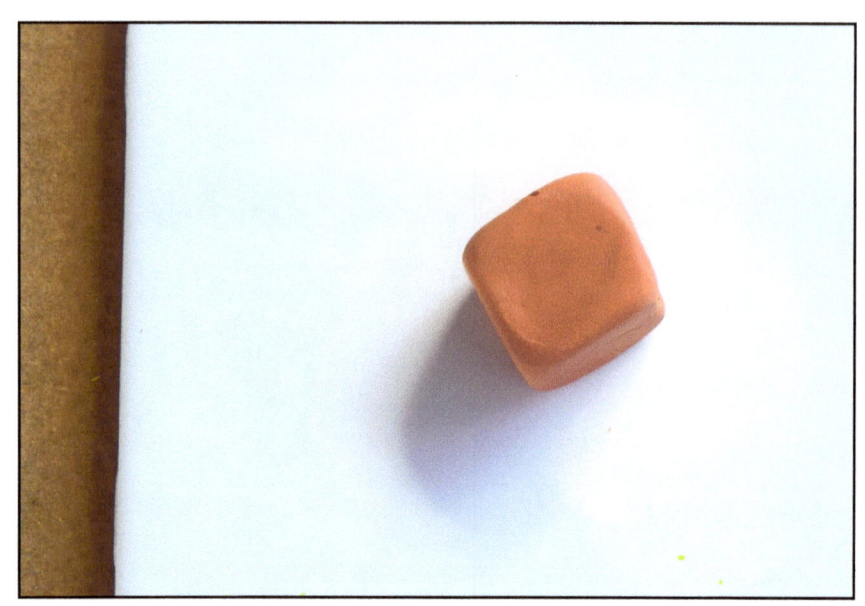

Cube
Square
Box

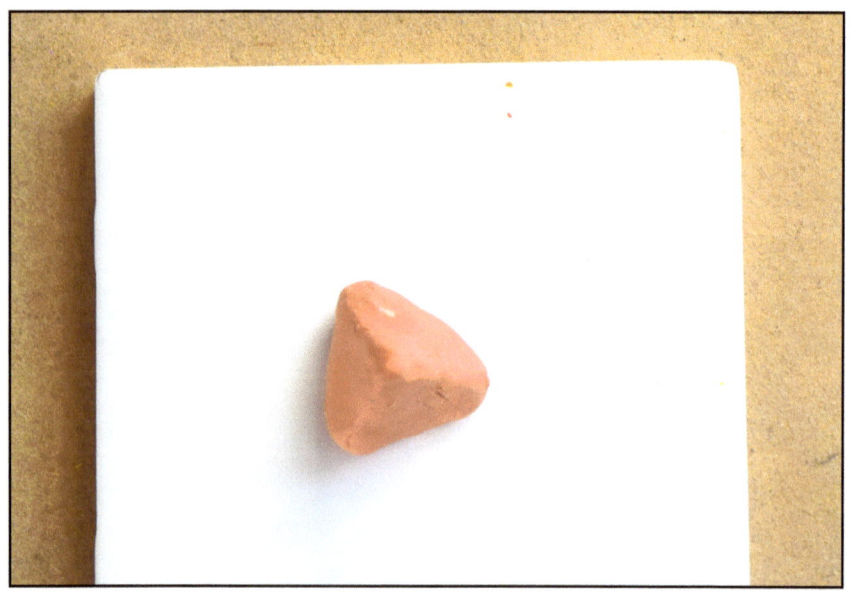

Pyramid
Triangle
Mountain Peak

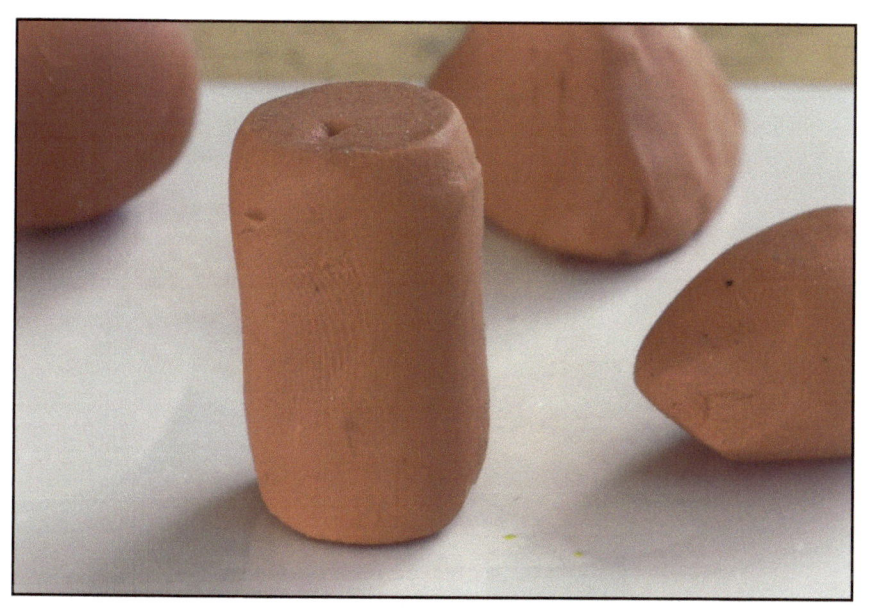

Cylinder

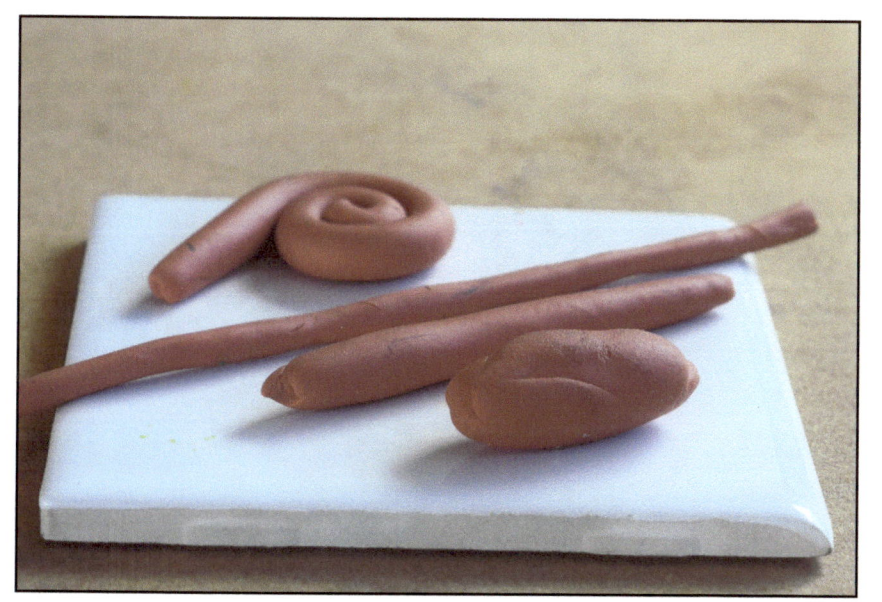

Ropelike Coils
Snakes

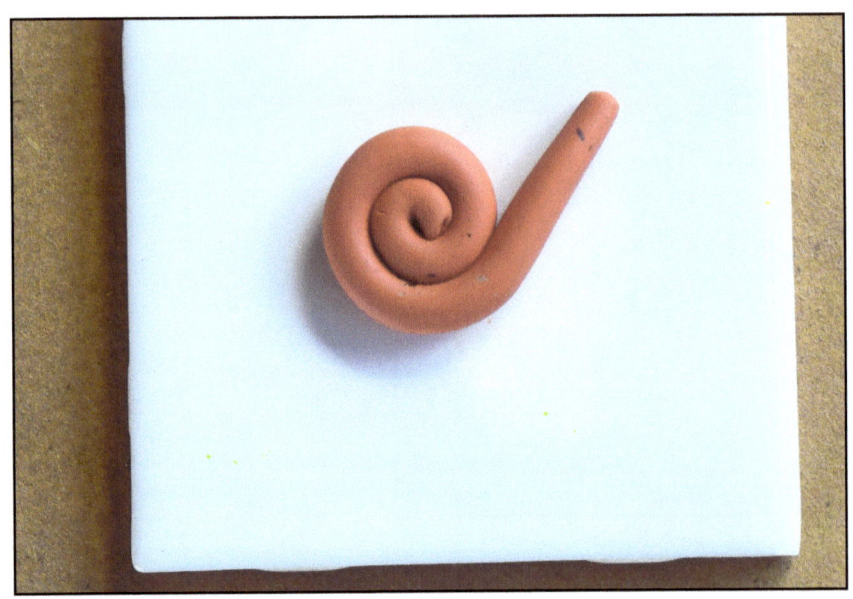

Coil

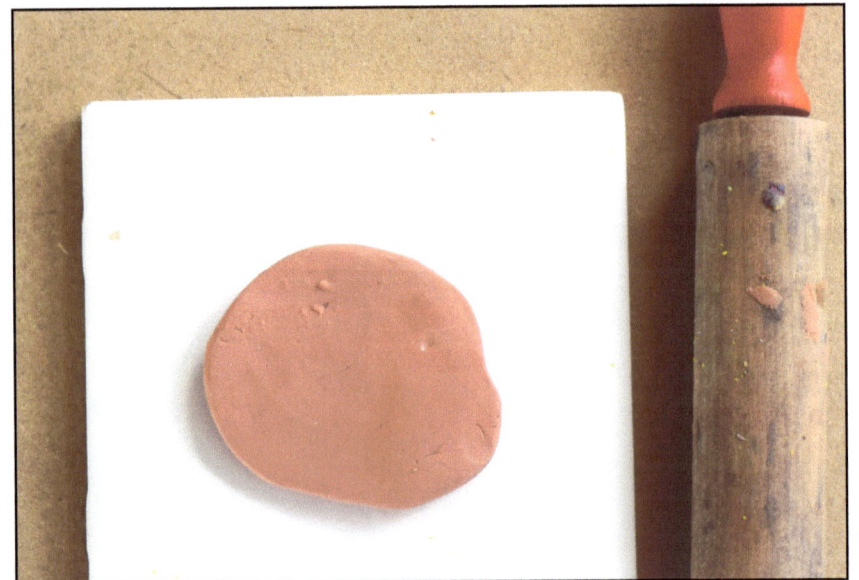

Flat Pancake

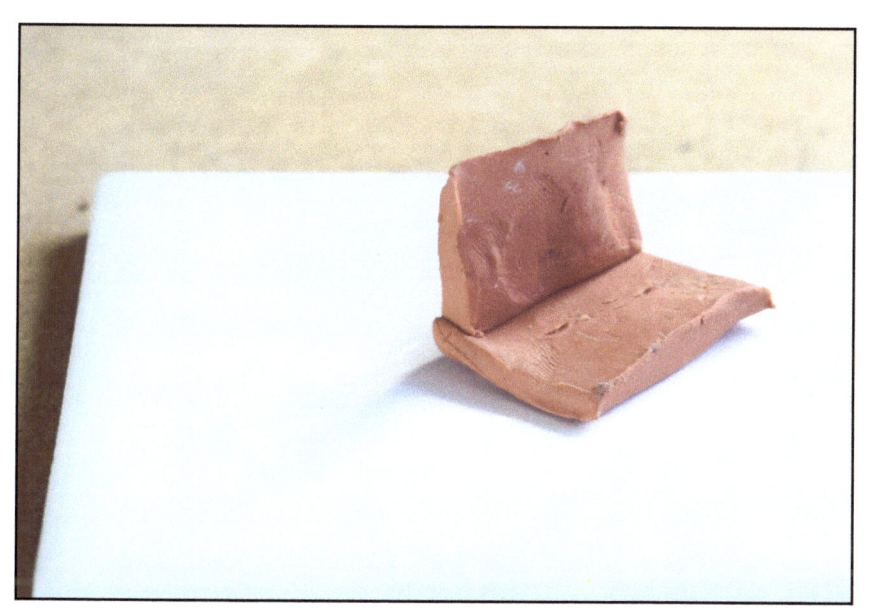

Slab
Slabs Attached

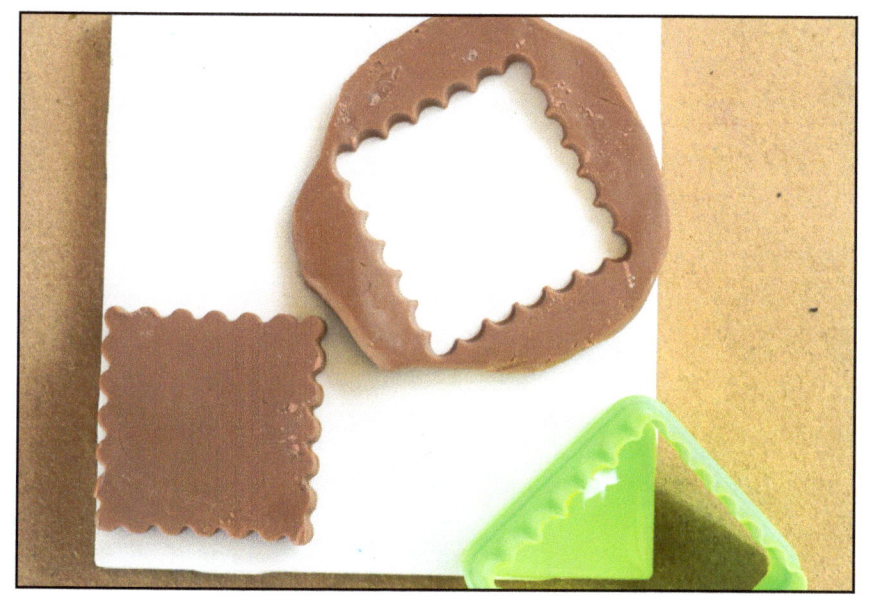

Cookie Cutter
Shapes

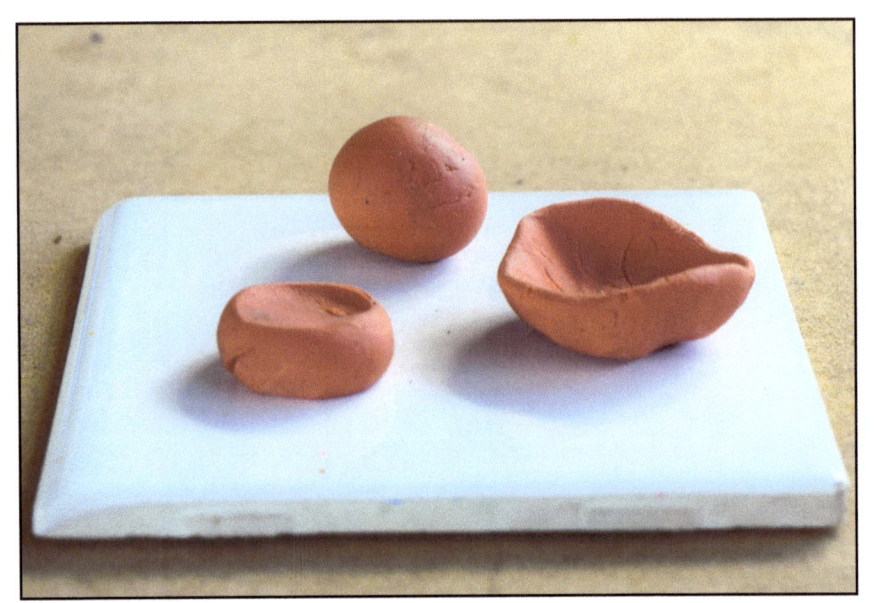

Pinch Pot
Bowl
Cup
Nest

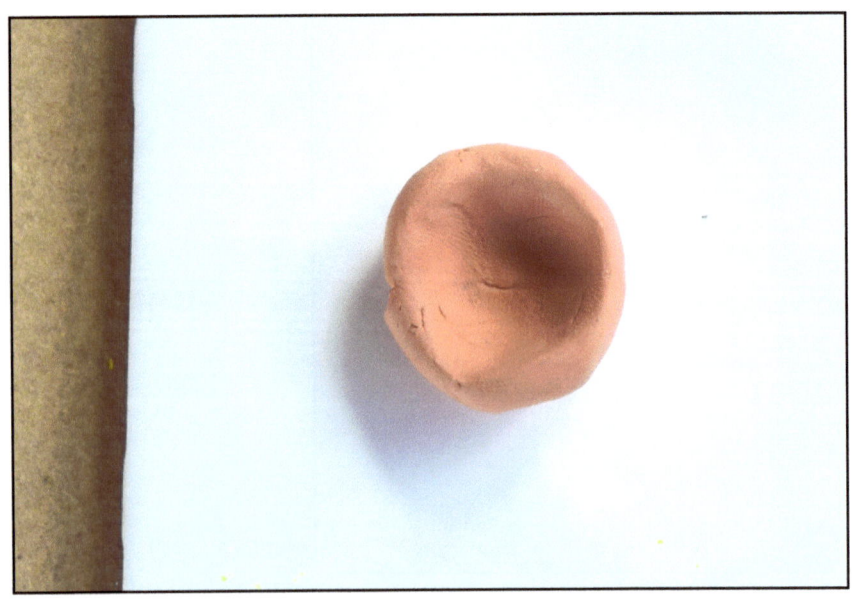

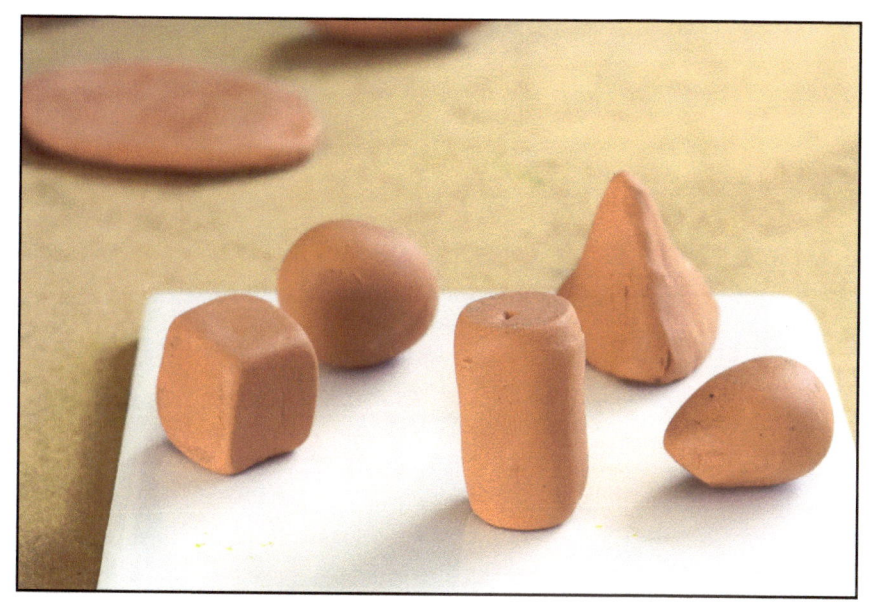

Sphere
Cube
Cylinder
Pyramid

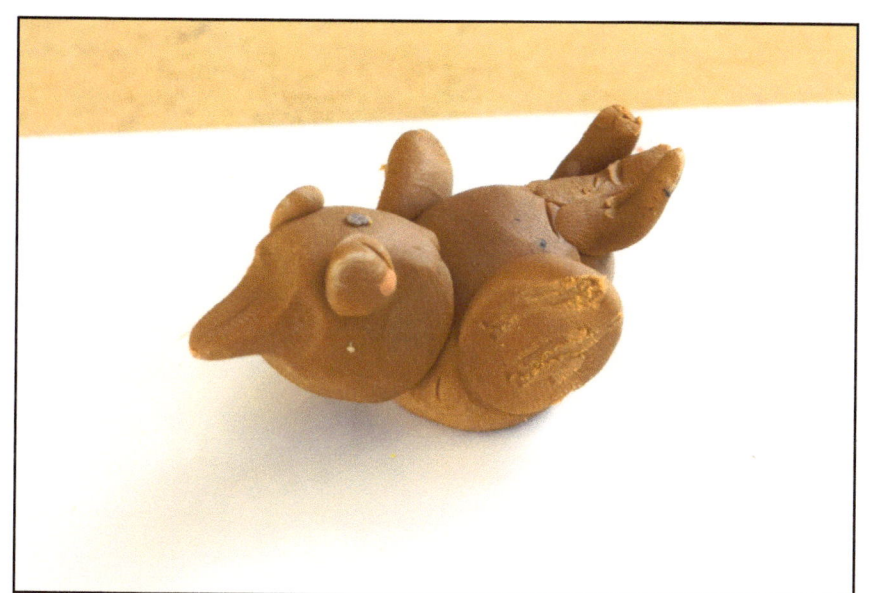

Attached Parts
Bird

31

Beginner Modeling Building Projects

Cookie Cutters Forms

Making shapes from cookie cutters is easy for first timers. All you need is a variety of cookie cutter shapes. Shapes can be embellished with all the lovely items listed in this book. Start off with a wedge of clay as big as the child's fist. You also want to consider the cookie cutters size, be sure there's enough for cut out.

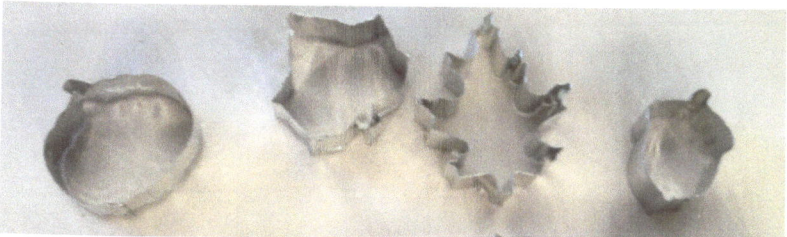

Steps:

1. Make a round ball by rolling on a table surface or between hands.

2. Flatten ball into pancake shape, then roll flat with rolling pin.

3. Press cookie cutter into clay, clear away extra clay around outside edges of cookie cutter shape and push cut shape out gently. This takes lots of practice.

4. Have child decorate by pressing and pushing embellishments into clay.

5. Use spatula to slide under forms to move to drying area. Using a spatula helps keep form together when moving them around. Pottery clay is very sticky and will usually stick to your surface the child is working on, so a spatula helps move and unstick to surfaces.

Note* 1/4 inch thick

The more a child presses and rolls out a slab it becomes thinner and wider. Too thin of a slab will be hard to pick up with spatula and can get ruined. Try to help kids keep slabs no thinner than a quarter of an inch. This takes practice and is part of exploring clays properties. You can roll out slabs and make cut out shapes for younger kids not fine motor ready. After awhile kids enjoy doing the whole process independently.

How to attach embellishments

Kids should see you press and push embellishments into clay. This is good for them to see with their own eyes the fun possibilities embellishments provide. This will give them a great understanding how shapes can be decorated. I recommend making several decorated shapes so they can see options and get inspired. This is also good for them to see how clay is sticky and how easy embellishments stay attached

Birds Nest

After kids have had a chance exploring cookie cutter shapes this project is great to follow up with. This project introduces hand building by forming and modeling clay pieces together. This is a two-part project making a bird and nest. You will start with forming a nest first. As art instructor I'm usually right next to kids demonstrating very slowly so they can build right along with me. If you have a large group, you will want some assistance to help younger kids struggling. These steps should be done very slowly so kids can keep up with you, pause so kids see every step. The idea is for kids to understand the basic building structure to making
simple form.

Steps:

Start off with a small wedge of clay half the size of a child's palm.

1. Form small ball by rolling on surface table or between hands.

2. Press thumb or index finger inside the middle of ball to start curve of bowl shape.

3. Squeeze sides with fingers to start forming small bird's nest. Kids should be pinching sides and pressing down in the middle to widen and deepen. The more pinching the child does, the more clay expands.

4. Ask child to set nest aside and start forming small items to be placed inside their newly formed nest, or fill up with embellishments. I usually ask kids to make tiny eggs to fill inside birds nest by rolling out several balls, they really enjoy doing this task, this is great tactile movements for perfecting ball forms.

Attaching Clay

Learning to attach pieces of clay parts together in advance hand building comes by scoring and slip techniques. For our beginning clay play we first start off by teaching kids to press and squeeze pieces together to attach them. Starting off with just hand forming, and later introducing tools to do more advance attachment techniques. Attaching embellishments into clay helps kids understand modeling and building ideas. Even making mound sculptures by sticking embellishments and twigs into clay is good learning you want to encourage.

Bird

This is great for introducing how to attach clay pieces together. Child will make five forms to attach together to make a small bird for their nest. Start off with very small pieces of clay. Look at the size of the nest and imagine the fully attached bird so you can estimate the piece sizes to start off with.

Steps:

1. Form a small ball by rolling on surface table or between hands, birds body base, set aside.

2. Roll another small ball smaller than the body, bird's head.

3. Next attach two balls together to form the basic bird body. Squeeze and press together smaller ball to body base, you should two balls attached together.

4. Next make two smaller balls to attach as wings on each side of the body base. Once balls are made flatten like tiny pancakes which become wings, press and squeeze onto each side
of body base.

5. After wings are attached, tell kids to add facial features like eyes and a beak. Remind kids to start eye forms like tiny balls. Almost every form starts with a ball!

6. Ask kids if their bird can fit into the nest they created, if not have them repeat make a new nest. If kids get inspired to make other forms allow this. I recommend you continue making your bird so kids can see the process even if they go on to do something else with their clay pieces. I do not encourage forcing kids to make a bird if they want to make something else. This should be an inspirational prompt to understand how clay is malleable and formable and can be built up. Clay play should be child-led and not difficult, keep it simple.

Authors Page

Additional Book Orders/Website Links

Email orders: treepassion@gmail.com
Telephone orders: U.S. (760) 652-5194
Postal Orders: P.O. Box 443, Solana Beach, CA 92075

Order Online: http://www.ecokidsart.com

Youtube: http://www.youtube.com/user/ecokidsart

Facebook: https://www.facebook.com/nature.of.art

Twitter: https://twitter.com/ecokidsart

Pinterest: http://www.pinterest.com/ecokidsart/
Google +: Spramani Elaun

Also avaliable as an e-Book
Nature of Art For Kids® Publishing
Go to www.EcoKidsArt.com

Order Other Books by Spramani Elaun:

Nurturing Children in The Visual Arts Naturally©
Kids Painting©
Kids Color Theory©
Introducing Visual Arts to The Montessori Classrooms©
Teaching Homeschool Visual Arts©
Kids Doodling & Drawing©
Early Childhood Education Visual Arts©

Learn More About Speaking/Seminars/Teacher Training/Conferences/Kids Zone Live Events:
http://www.ecokidsart.comor email: treepassion@gmail.com

Order Acrylic Paints, Watercolor Finger Paints, Painting & Drawing Supplies: http://www.ecokidsart.com

Order Colour Blocks Handcrafted Square Block Recycled Crayons: http://www.colourblocks.com